HIGH CALORIE RECIPES

FOR WEIGHT GAIN

50+ DELICIOUS HIGH CALORIE MEALS ANYONE CAN CONSUME FOR A HEALTHY WEIGHT GAIN IN NO TIME

RACHELLE K. SANDERS

COPYRIGHT

DISCLAIMER

Other books within the series

Stick to Thick

High Calorie Smoothie Recipes for Weight Gain

TABLE OF CONTENTS

BREAKFAST RECIPES

RECIPE ONE

CARROT CAKE OVERNIGHT OATMEAL

A delicious and healthy breakfast option that combines the flavors of carrot cake with hearty oats for a filling and satisfying morning meal.

INGREDIENTS:

1/2 cup old-fashioned rolled oats

1/2 cup grated carrot

1/2 cup unsweetened almond milk (or milk of choice)

1/4 cup plain Greek yogurt

1 tablespoon pure maple syrup

1/2 teaspoon vanilla extract

1/4 teaspoon ground cinnamon

1/8 teaspoon ground ginger

1/8 teaspoon ground nutmeg

Pinch of salt

Chopped nuts, raisins, banana slices, or shredded coconut (optional toppings)

INSTRUCTIONS:

1. In a medium-sized bowl, combine the oats, grated carrot, almond milk, Greek yogurt, maple syrup, vanilla extract, cinnamon, ginger, nutmeg, and salt. Stir well to combine.
2. Cover the bowl with plastic wrap and refrigerate overnight, or for at least 6 hours.
3. In the morning, give the oatmeal a good stir. If it seems too thick, you can add a splash more almond milk to thin it out.
4. Divide the oatmeal between two bowls, and sprinkle with any desired toppings.

NUTRITIONAL INFORMATION:

This recipe makes two servings. The following nutritional information is per serving:

Calories: 195, Total Fat: 4g, Saturated Fat: 0.5g, Cholesterol: 1mg, Sodium: 118mg, Total Carbohydrates: 33g, Dietary Fiber: 5g, Sugars: 11g, Protein: 9g.

PREP TIME:

The prep time for this recipe is about 5-10 minutes, plus at least 6 hours of chilling time in the refrigerator.

RECIPE TWO

CROISSANT BREAKFAST SANDWICH

A classic breakfast sandwich with a French twist - buttery croissants stuffed with eggs, cheese, and your choice of protein.

INGREDIENTS:

2 large croissants, halved

4 slices of bacon

4 large eggs

4 slices of cheddar cheese

2 tablespoons unsalted butter

Salt and pepper to taste

Optional: sliced avocado, tomato, or greens for toppings

INSTRUCTIONS:

1. Preheat the oven to 350°F.
2. In a skillet over medium heat, cook the bacon until crispy. Remove the bacon from the skillet and set aside on a paper towel-lined plate.
3. In the same skillet, melt 1 tablespoon of butter over medium heat. Crack the eggs into the skillet and season with salt and pepper. Cook until the whites are set and the yolks are still runny.
4. Meanwhile, place the croissant halves on a baking sheet, cut side up. Toast in the preheated oven for 5-7 minutes until lightly golden brown.
5. Once the croissants are toasted, remove from the oven and top the bottom half of each croissant with a slice of cheddar cheese, a slice of bacon, and a cooked egg. Top with any desired toppings, such as sliced avocado, tomato, or greens.
6. Place the top half of the croissant on each sandwich and spread a little butter on top. Place the sandwiches back in the oven and bake for 2-3 minutes until the cheese is melted and the croissant is golden brown.

NUTRITIONAL INFORMATION:

The following nutritional information is for one sandwich:

Calories: 595, Total Fat: 43g, Saturated Fat: 22g, Cholesterol: 385mg, Sodium: 822mg

Total Carbohydrates: 24g, Dietary Fiber: 1g, Sugars: 3g, Protein: 25g.

PREP TIME:

The prep time for this recipe is about 20 minutes.

RECIPE THREE

CHICKPEA SALAD

A protein-packed breakfat/lunch option made with chickpeas, veggies, and a t angy dressing.

INGREDIENTS:

2 cans (15 ounces each) chickpeas, drained and rinsed

1 red bell pepper, diced

1 yellow bell pepper, diced

1/2 red onion, diced

1 English cucumber, diced

1/4 cup chopped fresh parsley

1/4 cup chopped fresh mint

1/4 cup extra-virgin olive oil

2 tablespoons lemon juice

1 garlic clove, minced

1/2 teaspoon ground cumin

Salt and freshly ground black pepper, to taste

INSTRUCTIONS:

1. In a large bowl, combine the chickpeas, diced red and yellow bell peppers, diced red onion, diced English cucumber, chopped parsley, and chopped mint.
2. In a small bowl, whisk together the olive oil, lemon juice, minced garlic, ground cumin, salt, and pepper.
3. Pour the dressing over the chickpea salad and toss well to combine.
4. Cover the bowl with plastic wrap and refrigerate for at least 30 minutes before serving to allow the flavors to mel together.

NUTRITIONAL INFORMATION:

This recipe makes six servings. The following nutritional information is per serving:

Calories: 258, Total Fat: 12g, Saturated Fat: 1.5g, Cholesterol: 0mg, Sodium: 17mg, Total Carbohydrates: 31g, Dietary Fiber: 8g, Sugars: 6g, Protein: 9g.

PREP TIME:

The prep time for this recipe is about 20 minutes, plus at least 30 minutes of chilling time in the refrigerator.

RECIPE FOUR

VEGAN PROTEIN SALAD

A plant-based breakfast or lunch option loaded with healthy ingredients like quinoa, avocado, and veggies for a satisfying meal.

INGREDIENTS:

1/2 cup old-fashioned rolled oats

1/2 cup grated carrot

1/2 cup unsweetened almond milk (or milk of choice)

1/4 cup plain Greek yogurt

1 tablespoon pure maple syrup

1/2 teaspoon vanilla extract

1/4 teaspoon ground cinnamon

1/8 teaspoon ground ginger

1/8 teaspoon ground nutmeg

Pinch of salt

Chopped nuts, raisins, banana slices, or shredded coconut (optional toppings)

INSTRUCTIONS:

1. In a medium-sized bowl, combine the oats, grated carrot, almond milk, Greek yogurt, maple syrup, vanilla extract, cinnamon, ginger, nutmeg, and salt. Stir well to combine.
2. Cover the bowl with plastic wrap and refrigerate overnight, or for at least 6 hours.
3. In the morning, give the oatmeal a good stir. If it seems too thick, you can add a splash more almond milk to thin it out.
4. Divide the oatmeal between two bowls, and sprinkle with any desired toppings.

NUTRITIONAL INFORMATION:

This recipe makes two servings. The following nutritional information is per serving:

Calories: 195, Total Fat: 4g, Saturated Fat: 0.5g, Cholesterol: 1mg, Sodium: 118mg, Total Carbohydrates: 33g, Dietary Fiber: 5g, Sugars: 11g, Protein: 9g.

PREP TIME:

The prep time for this recipe is about 5-10 minutes, plus at least 6 hours of chilling time in the refrigerator.

RECIPE FIVE

KETO PORK PIE

A low-carb and high-fat meal option made with ground pork, almond flour crust, and keto-friendly seasonings.

INGREDIENTS:

2 cups almond flour

1/2 cup coconut flour

1/4 cup psyllium husk powder

1/4 cup flaxseed meal

1/2 teaspoon salt

1/2 teaspoon xanthan gum

1/2 cup unsalted butter, cold and cut into small pieces

1 large egg

1-2 tablespoons cold water, as needed

1 pound ground pork

1/2 onion, chopped

2 cloves garlic, minced

1/2 teaspoon dried thyme

1/2 teaspoon dried sage

1/2 teaspoon dried rosemary

1/4 teaspoon black pepper

1/4 teaspoon salt

1/4 cup chicken broth

1 large egg, beaten for egg wash

INSTRUCTIONS:

1. In a large bowl, whisk together the almond flour, coconut flour, psyllium husk powder, flaxseed meal, salt, and xanthan gum.
2. Add the cold butter pieces and use your hands or a pastry cutter to work the butter into the flour mixture until it resembles coarse crumbs.
3. Beat the egg in a separate small bowl, then add it to the flour mixture and stir until it forms a crumbly dough. If the dough is too dry, add water, 1 tablespoon at a time, until it comes together.
4. Divide the dough into two equal portions, one slightly larger than the other. Press the larger portion into the bottom and up the sides of a 9-inch pie dish to form the crust.
5. Preheat the oven to 375°F.
6. In a large skillet over medium-high heat, cook the ground pork, onion, and garlic until the pork is browned and the onion is translucent. Drain any excess fat.
7. Add the thyme, sage, rosemary, black pepper, salt, and chicken broth to the skillet. Cook, stirring frequently, until the broth has mostly evaporated and the mixture is thick and cohesive.
8. Pour the pork mixture into the pie crust and spread it out evenly.
9. Roll out the remaining dough on a sheet of parchment paper or silicone mat into a circle big

KETO PORK PIE (CONT'D)

enough to cover the top of the pie. Place it over the filling and press the edges together to seal.

10. Brush the top of the pie with the beaten egg, then cut a few small slits in the top to allow steam to escape.
11. Bake for 35-40 minutes, or until the crust is golden brown and the filling is hot and bubbly.
12. Let the pie cool for 10 minutes before slicing and serving

NUTRITIONAL INFORMATION:

This recipe makes eight servings. The following nutritional information is per serving:

Calories: 394, Total Fat: 32g, Saturated Fat: 11g, Cholesterol: 122mg, Sodium: 343mg, Total Carbohydrates: 10g, Dietary Fiber: 7g, Sugars: 2g, Protein: 18g.

PREP TIME:

The prep time for this recipe is about 30 minutes, and the bake time is about 40 minutes, for a total of 1 hour and 10 minutes.

RECIPE SIX

BAKED CHICKEN AND RICE

An easy meal option with juicy baked chicken served over a bed of fluffy rice.

INGREDIENTS:

4 bone-in, skin-on chicken thighs

1 cup long-grain white rice

2 cups chicken broth

1 medium onion, chopped

2 cloves garlic, minced

1 teaspoon dried thyme

1 teaspoon paprika

1/2 teaspoon salt

1/4 teaspoon black pepper

2 tablespoons olive oil

Lemon wedges, for serving

INSTRUCTIONS:

1. Preheat the oven to 375°F (190°C).
2. Rinse the chicken thighs and pat them dry with paper towels. Season them with salt, black pepper, and paprika.
3. Heat the olive oil in a large skillet over medium-high heat. Once the oil is hot, add the chicken thighs skin-side down and cook until the skin is golden brown and crispy, about 5 minutes. Flip the chicken and cook for another 2-3 minutes. Remove the chicken from the skillet and set aside.
4. Add the chopped onion and minced garlic to the skillet and cook until the onion is translucent, about 3-4 minutes.
5. Add the rice to the skillet and stir until the rice is coated in the onion and garlic mixture.
6. Add the chicken broth, dried thyme, salt, and black pepper to the skillet and stir to combine.
7. Bring the mixture to a simmer, then remove the skillet from the heat.
8. Transfer the rice mixture to a 9x13-inch baking dish.
9. Arrange the chicken thighs on top of the rice mixture, skin-side up.
10. Cover the baking dish with aluminum foil and bake for 45-50 minutes, or until the chicken is cooked through and the rice is tender.

BAKED CHICKEN AND RICE (CONT'D)

11. Remove the foil and bake for an additional 10-15 minutes, or until the chicken skin is crispy and golden brown.
12. Serve with lemon wedges on the side.

NUTRITIONAL INFORMATION:

This recipe makes 4 servings. The following nutritional information is per serving:

Calories: 480, Total Fat: 23g, Saturated Fat: 5g, Cholesterol: 103mg, Sodium: 845mg, Total Carbohydrates: 39g, Dietary Fiber: 1g, Sugars: 2g, Protein: 28g.

PREP TIME:

The prep time for this recipe is about 15 minutes, and the cooking time is approximately 1 hour

RECIPE SEVEN

VEGAN PESTO PASTA

A delicious and flavorful pasta dish made with a homemade vegan pesto sauce and your choice of veggies.

INGREDIENTS:

8 ounces of your favorite pasta (gluten-free if needed)

2 cups packed fresh basil leaves

2 garlic cloves, peeled

1/4 cup pine nuts (or walnuts)

1/4 cup nutritional yeast

1/4 cup extra-virgin olive oil

1/4 teaspoon sea salt

Freshly ground black pepper, to taste

INSTRUCTIONS:

1. Cook pasta according to package directions. Drain and set aside.
2. In a food processor, combine basil, garlic, pine nuts, nutritional yeast, and sea salt. Pulse until the ingredients are roughly chopped.
3. While the food processor is running, slowly add the olive oil in a steady stream until the mixture is smooth.
4. In a large bowl, combine the cooked pasta with the pesto sauce. Toss until the pasta is evenly coated with the sauce.
5. Season with freshly ground black pepper to taste.
6. Serve warm, topped with extra pine nuts or nutritional yeast, if desired.

NUTRITIONAL INFORMATION:

This recipe makes four servings. The following nutritional information is per serving:

Calories: 407, Total Fat: 22g, Saturated Fat: 3g, Cholesterol: 0mg, Sodium: 190mg, Total Carbohydrates: 44g, Dietary Fiber: 4g, Sugars: 2g, Protein: 10g

PREP TIME:

The prep time for this recipe is about 15 minutes, and the cooking time for the pasta varies based on the type of pasta used. Plan for an additional 10-12 minutes to cook the pasta

RECIPE EIGHT

CHICKEN AL FREDO BAKE

A classic Italian-inspired dinner option with tender chicken, al dente pasta, and a creamy Alfredo sauce.

INGREDIENTS:

8 oz penne pasta

2 cups cooked and shredded chicken breast

2 cups Alfredo sauce

1/2 cup shredded Parmesan cheese

1 cup shredded mozzarella cheese

2 cloves garlic, minced

1/4 cup chopped fresh parsley

Salt and black pepper to taste

INSTRUCTIONS:

1. Preheat your oven to 375°F (190°C) and grease a 9x13 inch baking dish.
2. Cook the penne pasta according to the package directions until al dente. Drain and set aside.
3. In a large bowl, combine the cooked pasta, shredded chicken, Alfredo sauce, Parmesan cheese, minced garlic, chopped parsley, salt, and black pepper. Stir until everything is evenly combined.
4. Pour the pasta mixture into the prepared baking dish and spread it out evenly.
5. Sprinkle the shredded mozzarella cheese over the top of the pasta mixture.
6. Bake the chicken Alfredo bake for 20-25 minutes, or until the cheese is melted and bubbly and the edges are lightly browned.
7. Let the dish cool for a few minutes before serving. Garnish with additional chopped parsley if desired.

NUTRITIONAL INFORMATION:

This recipe makes about 6 servings. The following nutritional information is per serving:

Calories: 475, Total Fat: 28g, Saturated Fat: 14g, Cholesterol: 98mg, Sodium: 687mg, Total Carbohydrates: 28g, Dietary Fiber: 1g, Sugars: 2g, Protein: 27g.

PREP TIME:

The prep time for this recipe is about 20-25 minutes, and the bake time is also 20-25 minutes. So, the total time needed for this recipe is about 45-50 minutes.

RECIPE NINE

SALMON WITH VEGGIES

A healthy dinner option with pan-seared salmon served over a bed of roasted veggies.

INGREDIENTS:

2 salmon fillets, skin-on

2 cups mixed vegetables (e.g. broccoli, carrots, bell peppers, zucchini), chopped

2 tablespoons olive oil

1/2 teaspoon garlic powder

1/2 teaspoon paprika

1/4 teaspoon salt

1/4 teaspoon black pepper

Lemon wedges, for serving

INSTRUCTIONS:

1. Preheat the oven to 400°F (200°C). Line a baking sheet with parchment paper.
2. In a large bowl, toss the mixed vegetables with 1 tablespoon of olive oil, garlic powder, paprika, salt, and black pepper. Mix until the vegetables are evenly coated.
3. Arrange the seasoned vegetables in a single layer on the prepared baking sheet.
4. Place the salmon fillets, skin-side down, on top of the vegetables.
5. Drizzle the remaining 1 tablespoon of olive oil over the salmon fillets.
6. Bake for 12-15 minutes, until the salmon is cooked through and the vegetables are tender and lightly browned.
7. Serve hot with lemon wedges.

NUTRITIONAL INFORMATION:

This recipe makes two servings. The following nutritional information is per serving:

Calories: 392, Total Fat: 25g, Saturated Fat: 4g, Cholesterol: 62mg, Sodium: 340mg, Total Carbohydrates: 11g, Dietary Fiber: 4g, Sugars: 4g, Protein: 31g

PREP TIME:

The prep time for this recipe is about 15 minutes, and the cooking time is 12-15 minutes. So, you can have a delicious, healthy meal on the table in less than 30 minutes!

LUNCHE RECIPES

RECIPE TEN

CHICKEN SHAWARMA QUINOA BOWL

A Mediterranean-inspired lunch option made with quinoa, spiced chicken, and veggies for a filling and flavorful meal.

INGREDIENTS:

For the Chicken Shawarma:

1 lb boneless, skinless chicken thighs, cut into bite-sized pieces

2 tablespoons olive oil

2 tablespoons lemon juice

2 teaspoons ground cumin

2 teaspoons smoked paprika

1 teaspoon ground turmeric

1/2 teaspoon ground cinnamon

1/4 teaspoon ground cardamom

Salt and freshly ground black pepper, to taste

For the Quinoa Bowl:

1 cup uncooked quinoa, rinsed and drained

2 cups low-sodium chicken broth

1 can chickpeas, drained and rinsed

1 red onion, sliced

1 red bell pepper, sliced

1 yellow bell pepper, sliced

1/4 cup chopped fresh parsley

1/4 cup chopped fresh mint

1/4 cup chopped fresh cilantro

1/4 cup chopped roasted almonds

1/4 cup crumbled feta cheese

Lemon wedges, for serving

INSTRUCTIONS:

For the Chicken Shawarma:

1. In a large bowl, whisk together the olive oil, lemon juice, cumin, smoked paprika, turmeric, cinnamon, and cardamom.
2. Add the chicken to the bowl and toss to coat with the marinade. Season with salt and pepper.
3. Cover the bowl and refrigerate for at least 30 minutes, or up to 4 hours.
4. Heat a large skillet over medium-high heat. Add the chicken and cook until browned and cooked through, about 6-8 minutes.

CHICKEN SHAWARMA QUINOA BOWL (CONT'D)

INSTRUCTIONS:

For the Quinoa Bowl:

1. In a medium saucepan, combine the quinoa and chicken broth. Bring to a boil, then reduce the heat to low and simmer, covered, for 15-20 minutes or until the liquid is absorbed and the quinoa is cooked.
2. In a large bowl, combine the cooked quinoa, chickpeas, sliced red onion, red and yellow bell peppers, chopped parsley, mint, and cilantro.
3. Divide the quinoa mixture among four bowls. Top each bowl with some of the cooked chicken shawarma, chopped roasted almonds, and crumbled feta cheese.
4. Serve with lemon wedges on the side.

NUTRITIONAL INFORMATION:

This recipe makes 4 servings. The following nutritional information is per serving:

Calories: 530, Total Fat: 24g, Saturated Fat: 5g, Cholesterol: 95mg, Sodium: 290mg, Total Carbohydrates: 44g, Dietary Fiber: 10g, Sugars: 5g, Protein: 35g.

PREP TIME:

The prep time for this recipe is about 20-30 minutes, plus time for marinating the chicken and cooking the quinoa.

RECIPE ELEVEN

HERB CHICKEN COUSCOUS

A light and flavorful lunch/dinner option with herb-seasoned chicken served over fluffy couscous.

INGREDIENTS:

2 boneless, skinless chicken breasts, cut into 1-inch pieces

1 tablespoon olive oil

1 teaspoon dried thyme

1 teaspoon dried oregano

1/2 teaspoon garlic powder

1/2 teaspoon onion powder

1/2 teaspoon salt

1/4 teaspoon black pepper

1 cup whole wheat couscous

1 and 1/2 cups low-sodium chicken broth

2 tablespoons chopped fresh parsley

2 tablespoons chopped fresh mint

1 tablespoon chopped fresh dill

1 lemon, cut into wedges (optional, for serving)

INSTRUCTIONS:

1. In a large skillet, heat the olive oil over medium-high heat. Add the chicken pieces and sprinkle with the thyme, oregano, garlic powder, onion powder, salt, and black pepper. Cook for 6-8 minutes, or until the chicken is browned and cooked through.
2. While the chicken is cooking, prepare the couscous according to the package directions, using the chicken broth instead of water.
3. Once the couscous is cooked, fluff it with a fork and stir in the chopped parsley, mint, and dill.
4. Serve the couscous topped with the cooked chicken and a squeeze of fresh lemon juice, if desired.

NUTRITIONAL INFORMATION:

This recipe makes four servings. The following nutritional information is per serving:

Calories: 355, Total Fat: 6g, Saturated Fat: 1g, Cholesterol: 52mg, Sodium: 405mg, Total Carbohydrates: 46g, Dietary Fiber: 6g, Sugars: 1g, Protein: 31g.

PREP TIME:

The prep time for this recipe is about 10 minutes, and the cooking time is about 15 minutes.

MUSHROOM CARNITAS BOWL

A vegetarian lunch option made with meaty mushrooms, black beans, and fresh toppings for a tasty and filling meal.

INGREDIENTS:

For the Mushroom Carnitas:

1 pound mushrooms, sliced (such as shiitake, oyster, or portobello)

1 onion, sliced

4 cloves garlic, minced

1 tablespoon olive oil

2 teaspoons chili powder

2 teaspoons cumin

1 teaspoon smoked paprika

1/2 teaspoon salt

Juice of 1 lime

For the Bowl:

1 cup cooked brown rice

1 can black beans, drained and rinsed

1 avocado, sliced

1/4 cup chopped fresh cilantro

1 lime, cut into wedges

Hot sauce, to taste

INSTRUCTIONS:

1. Heat the olive oil in a large skillet over medium heat. Add the sliced mushrooms, onion, and garlic, and cook until the mushrooms have released their moisture and are lightly browned, stirring occasionally, about 10-12 minutes.
2. Add the chili powder, cumin, smoked paprika, and salt to the skillet, and stir to combine. Cook for an additional 2-3 minutes, or until the spices are fragrant.
3. Remove the skillet from the heat, and stir in the lime juice.
4. To assemble the bowls, divide the cooked rice between two bowls. Top each bowl with half of the mushroom carnitas and black beans.
5. Add the sliced avocado and chopped cilantro to each bowl.
6. Serve with lime wedges and hot sauce, if desired.

NUTRITIONAL INFORMATION:

This recipe makes two servings. The following nutritional information is per serving:

Calories: 573, Total Fat: 26g, Saturated Fat: 3.5g, Cholesterol: 0mg, Sodium: 662mg, Total Carbohydrates: 74g, Dietary Fiber: 25g, Sugars: 6g, Protein: 21g.

PREP TIME:

The prep time for this recipe is about 10-15 minutes, and the cook time is about 15 minutes.

RECIPE THIRTEEN

RED KIDNEY BEAN BURGER BOWL

A plant-based lunch option with homemade bean burgers served over a bed of greens and topped with your favorite toppings.

INGREDIENTS:

For the burgers:

1 can (15 oz) red kidney beans, drained and rinsed

1/2 cup cooked quinoa

1/2 cup breadcrumbs

1/4 cup diced red onion

1/4 cup chopped fresh parsley

1 egg, beaten

2 cloves garlic, minced

1 tablespoon olive oil

1/2 teaspoon ground cumin

1/2 teaspoon chili powder

1/2 teaspoon smoked paprika

Salt and pepper, to taste

For the bowl:

2 cups cooked brown rice

2 cups mixed salad greens

1 avocado, sliced

1/4 cup crumbled feta cheese

2 tablespoons chopped fresh cilantro

Lime wedges, for serving

INSTRUCTIONS:

1. In a large bowl, mash the kidney beans with a fork until they are mostly broken down.
2. Add the cooked quinoa, breadcrumbs, red onion, parsley, egg, garlic, olive oil, cumin, chili powder, smoked paprika, salt, and pepper to the bowl. Stir everything together until well combined.
3. Use your hands to form the mixture into four evenly-sized burger patties.
4. Heat a large non-stick skillet over medium-high heat. Add the burgers to the skillet and cook for 3-4 minutes per side, or until they are browned and crispy on the outside.
5. While the burgers are cooking, prepare the rest of the bowl. Divide the cooked brown rice between two bowls, then top each bowl with salad greens, sliced avocado, and crumbled feta cheese.
6. When the burgers are finished cooking, place two burgers on top of each bowl.
7. Garnish each bowl with chopped cilantro and serve with lime wedges.

RED KIDNEY BEAN BURGER BOWL (CONT'D)

NUTRITIONAL INFORMATION:

This recipe makes two servings. The following nutritional information is per serving:

Calories: 702, Total Fat: 34g, Saturated Fat: 8g, Cholesterol: 97mg, Sodium: 812mg, Total Carbohydrates: 79g, Dietary Fiber: 18g, Sugars: 4g, Protein: 25g.

PREP TIME:

The prep time for this recipe is about 20 minutes, and the cook time is about 10 minutes.

CHICKEN FARRO SALAD

A hearty and healthy lunch option made with farro, grilled chicken, and fresh veggies.

INGREDIENTS:

1 cup uncooked farro

2 cups water

1/2 teaspoon salt

2 cups cooked, shredded chicken breast

1 large cucumber, diced

1 large red bell pepper, diced

1/4 cup chopped fresh parsley

1/4 cup chopped fresh mint

1/4 cup chopped fresh chives

1/4 cup crumbled feta cheese

1/4 cup toasted pine nuts

1/4 cup extra-virgin olive oil

3 tablespoons fresh lemon juice

1 garlic clove, minced

Salt and freshly ground black pepper, to taste

INSTRUCTIONS:

1. Rinse the farro in cold water and drain well. In a medium saucepan, bring the farro, water, and salt to a boil. Reduce heat to low, cover, and simmer until the farro is tender but still chewy, about 20-25 minutes. Drain off any excess water and set aside to cool.
2. In a large bowl, combine the cooled farro, shredded chicken, cucumber, red bell pepper, parsley, mint, chives, feta cheese, and pine nuts. Toss well to combine.
3. In a small bowl, whisk together the olive oil, lemon juice, garlic, salt, and pepper until well combined. Pour the dressing over the salad and toss to coat.
4. Serve the salad immediately or chill in the refrigerator until ready to serve.

NUTRITIONAL INFORMATION:

This recipe makes about 4-6 servings. The following nutritional information is per serving:

Calories: 415, Total Fat: 23g, Saturated Fat: 4g, Cholesterol: 50mg, Sodium: 466mg, Total Carbohydrates: 31g, Dietary Fiber: 6g, Sugars: 4g, Protein: 25g.

PREP TIME:

The prep time for this recipe is about 15-20 minutes, plus about 25 minutes to cook the farro.ator.

RECIPE FIFTEEN

CHICKEN AVOCADO SALAD

A refreshing salad with tender chicken, creamy avocado, and crisp veggies for a light and healthy meal.

INGREDIENTS:

2 boneless, skinless chicken breasts

1/2 teaspoon garlic powder

1/2 teaspoon paprika

Salt and pepper to taste

4 cups mixed greens

1 avocado, diced

1/2 cup cherry tomatoes, halved

1/4 cup red onion, thinly sliced

1/4 cup crumbled feta cheese

2 tablespoons chopped fresh cilantro

2 tablespoons olive oil

1 tablespoon honey

1 tablespoon apple cider vinegar

1 tablespoon fresh lime juice

INSTRUCTIONS:

1. Preheat the oven to 375°F (190°C).
2. Season the chicken breasts with garlic powder, paprika, salt, and pepper.
3. Place the chicken on a baking sheet lined with parchment paper.
4. Bake the chicken for 20-25 minutes, or until the internal temperature reaches 165°F (75°C).
5. Let the chicken rest for 5-10 minutes, then slice it into strips.
6. In a large bowl, combine the mixed greens, diced avocado, cherry tomatoes, sliced red onion, crumbled feta cheese, and chopped cilantro.
7. In a separate small bowl, whisk together the olive oil, honey, apple cider vinegar, and lime juice to make the dressing.
8. Pour the dressing over the salad and toss to coat.
9. Top the salad with the sliced chicken and serve.

NUTRITIONAL INFORMATION:

This recipe makes two servings. The following nutritional information is per serving:

Calories: 490, Total Fat: 34g, Saturated Fat: 7g, Cholesterol: 89mg, Sodium: 368mg, Total Carbohydrates: 18g, Dietary Fiber: 7g, Sugars: 8g, Protein: 29g.

PREP TIME:

The prep time for this recipe is about 15-20 minutes, plus 20-25 minutes for cooking the chickenator.

RECIPE SIXTEEN

SLOPPY JOE CASSEROLE

A twist on a classic American favorite, made into a delicious and easy casserole with ground beef, veggies, and a flavorful sauce.

INGREDIENTS:

1 lb ground beef

1 small onion, chopped

1 green bell pepper, chopped

1 can (15 oz) sloppy joe sauce

1 can (14.5 oz) diced tomatoes, drained

1 can (8 oz) tomato sauce

1 cup shredded cheddar cheese

2 cups cooked elbow macaroni

1 tablespoon vegetable oil

Salt and pepper to taste

INSTRUCTIONS:

1. Preheat your oven to 375°F (190°C).
2. Heat the vegetable oil in a large skillet over medium-high heat. Add the onion and green pepper and cook until they are soft and fragrant.
3. Add the ground beef and cook until it is browned and cooked through. Drain any excess fat.
4. Add the sloppy joe sauce, diced tomatoes, and tomato sauce to the skillet. Stir everything together and season with salt and pepper to taste.
5. Add the cooked elbow macaroni to the skillet and stir until everything is combined.
6. Transfer the mixture to a greased 9x13 inch baking dish. Sprinkle the shredded cheddar cheese over the top.
7. Bake the casserole for 25-30 minutes, or until the cheese is melted and bubbly.
8. Let the casserole cool for a few minutes before serving.

NUTRITIONAL INFORMATION:

This recipe makes 8 servings. The following nutritional information is per serving:

Calories: 320, Total Fat: 16g, Saturated Fat: 7g, Cholesterol: 63mg, Sodium: 669mg, Total Carbohydrates: 20g, Dietary Fiber: 2g, Sugars: 9g, Protein: 23g.

PREP TIME:

The prep time for this recipe is about 15 minutes, and the cooking time is 25-30 minutes. So, the total time is around 40-45 minutesator.

DINNER RECIPES

RECIPE ONE

CHEESY CHICKEN NOODLE CASSEROLE

A comforting and cheesy dinner option with tender chicken, hearty noodles, and a creamy cheese sauce.

INGREDIENTS:

8 oz egg noodles

2 cups cooked and shredded chicken

1 cup frozen peas

1/2 cup diced onion

1/2 cup diced celery

1/2 cup diced carrots

2 cloves garlic, minced

2 tablespoons unsalted butter

2 tablespoons all-purpose flour

1 1/2 cups milk

1 cup shredded cheddar cheese

1/2 teaspoon salt

1/4 teaspoon black pepper

1/4 cup breadcrumbs

INSTRUCTIONS:

1. Preheat the oven to 375°F.
2. Cook the egg noodles according to package directions. Drain and set aside.
3. In a large saucepan, melt the butter over medium heat. Add the onion, celery, and carrots, and cook until the vegetables are tender, about 5-7 minutes. Add the garlic and cook for an additional 30 seconds.
4. Sprinkle the flour over the vegetables and stir to combine. Cook for 1-2 minutes, stirring constantly.
5. Slowly add the milk, whisking constantly to prevent lumps. Cook for 3-5 minutes, or until the sauce has thickened.
6. Stir in the shredded cheddar cheese, salt, and black pepper, and stir until the cheese has melted and the sauce is smooth.
7. Add the cooked egg noodles, shredded chicken, and frozen peas to the saucepan, and stir to combine.
8. Transfer the mixture to a 9x13 inch baking dish. Sprinkle the breadcrumbs evenly over the top.
9. Bake for 25-30 minutes, or until the casserole is hot and bubbly and the breadcrumbs are golden brown.

CHEESY CHICKEN NOODLE CASSEROLE(CONT'D)

NUTRITIONAL INFORMATION:

This recipe makes 8 servings. The following nutritional information is per serving:

Calories: 315, Total Fat: 13g, Saturated Fat: 7g, Cholesterol: 78mg, Sodium: 406mg, Total Carbohydrates: 26g, Dietary Fiber: 2g, Sugars: 4g, Protein: 22g.

PREP TIME:

The prep time for this recipe is about 30-40 minutes.

RECIPE TWO

KETO CROCKPOT CHICKEN

A low-carb and easy dinner option made in the crockpot with juicy chicken, cream cheese, and keto-friendly seasonings.

INGREDIENTS:

4 boneless, skinless chicken breasts

1 cup chicken broth

1/2 cup chopped onion

1/2 cup chopped celery

1/2 cup chopped bell pepper

1/4 cup tomato paste

2 cloves garlic, minced

2 tsp dried oregano

2 tsp paprika

1 tsp cumin

1/2 tsp salt

1/4 tsp black pepper

1/4 tsp cayenne pepper (optional)

2 tbsp olive oil

2 tbsp chopped fresh parsley (optional)

INSTRUCTIONS:

1. Add the chicken breasts to the crockpot and pour in the chicken broth.
2. In a skillet, heat the olive oil over medium-high heat. Add the onion, celery, and bell pepper and cook until the vegetables are soft and lightly browned, about 5-7 minutes.
3. Add the tomato paste, garlic, oregano, paprika, cumin, salt, black pepper, and cayenne pepper (if using) to the skillet. Stir until the tomato paste is fully incorporated into the vegetable mixture.
4. Pour the vegetable and spice mixture over the chicken breasts in the crockpot. Cover the crockpot and cook on low for 6-8 hours or on high for 3-4 hours, until the chicken is cooked through and tender.
5. Once the chicken is cooked, remove it from the crockpot and shred it with two forks.
6. Return the shredded chicken to the crockpot and stir to combine it with the cooking liquid and vegetable mixture.
7. Serve hot, garnished with chopped fresh parsley (if using).

NUTRITIONAL INFORMATION:

This recipe makes four servings. Each serving contains approximately:

295 calories, 14g fat, 5g carbohydrates, 1g fiber, 36g protein.

KETO CROCKPOT CHICKEN (CONT'D)

PREP TIME:

15 minutes (not including cooking time)

I hope you enjoy this Keto Crockpot Chicken recipe! It's a great option for a low-carb, high-protein meal that's easy to make and delicious.

RECIPE THREE

VEGAN PULLED JACKFRUIT SANDWICH

A plant-based lunch option with shredded jackfruit in a tangy BBQ sauce, served on a bun with your favorite toppings.

INGREDIENTS:

1 can (20 oz) young green jackfruit in brine or water, drained and rinsed

1/2 cup BBQ sauce

1/4 cup vegetable broth

1 tbsp olive oil

1/2 medium onion, diced

2 cloves garlic, minced

1/4 tsp smoked paprika

1/4 tsp chili powder

1/4 tsp cumin

Salt and pepper, to taste

4 hamburger buns

Optional toppings: coleslaw, sliced red onion, pickles

INSTRUCTIONS:

1. Preheat oven to 375°F.
2. Rinse and drain the jackfruit. Use a knife to remove the core and seeds, then use your hands or a fork to shred the jackfruit into small pieces.
3. In a small bowl, mix the BBQ sauce and vegetable broth together.
4. In a large skillet, heat olive oil over medium heat. Add onion and garlic and sauté until the onion is translucent and the garlic is fragrant, about 3-4 minutes.
5. Add the shredded jackfruit to the skillet, along with the BBQ sauce mixture, smoked paprika, chili powder, cumin, salt, and pepper. Stir well to combine.
6. Bring the mixture to a simmer, then reduce heat to low and let it cook for about 10 minutes, stirring occasionally.
7. While the jackfruit mixture is cooking, place the hamburger buns on a baking sheet and toast them in the preheated oven for 3-4 minutes.
8. When the jackfruit mixture is done cooking, remove it from the heat and let it cool for a few minutes.
9. To assemble the sandwiches, place a generous amount of the jackfruit mixture on each toasted hamburger bun. Top with coleslaw, sliced red onion, pickles, or any other toppings you like.

VEGAN PULLED JACKFRUIT SANDWICH (CONT'D)

NUTRITIONAL INFORMATION:

Calories: 317, Fat: 7g, Carbohydrates: 59g, Protein: 5g, Fiber: 6g.

PREP TIME: 15 MINUTES

COOK TIME: 15 MINUTES

Note: This recipe makes 4 sandwiches. Leftover jackfruit mixture can be stored in an airtight container in the refrigerator for up to 3 days.

RECIPE FOUR

CHICKEN PERI PERI

A flavorful and spicy dinner option with grilled chicken marinated in a zesty Peri Peri sauce.

INGREDIENTS:

4 boneless, skinless chicken breasts

3 tablespoons olive oil

2 tablespoons red wine vinegar

2 tablespoons paprika

2 tablespoons garlic powder

1 tablespoon cumin

1 tablespoon oregano

1 tablespoon salt

1 tablespoon black pepper

1 tablespoon crushed red pepper flakes

1 lemon, juiced

INSTRUCTIONS:

1. In a large mixing bowl, whisk together olive oil, red wine vinegar, paprika, garlic powder, cumin, oregano, salt, black pepper, crushed red pepper flakes, and lemon juice until combined.
2. Add chicken breasts to the mixing bowl and toss to coat them evenly with the marinade. Cover and refrigerate for at least 1 hour, or up to 24 hours.
3. Preheat the oven to 400°F (205°C).
4. Place the marinated chicken breasts in a baking dish and pour any remaining marinade over them.
5. Bake the chicken for 20-25 minutes or until fully cooked through, with an internal temperature of 165°F (74°C).
6. Remove the chicken from the oven and let it rest for 5 minutes before slicing and serving.

NUTRITIONAL INFORMATION:

Calories: 280, Protein: 28g, Fat: 14g, Carbohydrates: 7g, Fiber: 2g, Sugar: 1g, Sodium: 1350mg.

PREP TIME: **10 MINUTES**

COOK TIME: **25 MINUTES**

The prep time for this recipe is about 5-10 minutes, plus at least 6 hours of chilling time in the refrigerator.

RECIPE FIVE

CHICKEN THIGHS WITH BROCCOLI SALAD

This meal features tender and juicy chicken thighs roasted to perfection, served with a fresh and crunchy broccoli salad on the side. It's a healthy and satisfying combination of protein and veggies.

INGREDIENTS:

4 bone-in, skin-on chicken thighs

1 tbsp olive oil

1 tsp paprika

1 tsp garlic powder

Salt and pepper, to taste

2 cups broccoli florets

1/2 cup chopped red onion

1/2 cup chopped celery

1/4 cup chopped almonds

1/4 cup raisins

1/4 cup plain Greek yogurt

1 tbsp apple cider vinegar

1 tbsp honey

1 tsp Dijon mustard

INSTRUCTIONS:

1. Preheat the oven to 400°F.
2. In a small bowl, mix together the olive oil, paprika, garlic powder, salt, and pepper.
3. Rub the seasoning mixture all over the chicken thighs.
4. Place the chicken thighs on a baking sheet, skin-side up.
5. Roast the chicken thighs in the preheated oven for 30-35 minutes, until the skin is crispy and the internal temperature of the chicken reaches 165°F.
6. While the chicken is roasting, prepare the broccoli salad. In a large bowl, mix together the broccoli florets, chopped red onion, chopped celery, chopped almonds, and raisins.
7. In a small bowl, whisk together the Greek yogurt, apple cider vinegar, honey, and Dijon mustard.
8. Pour the dressing over the broccoli salad and toss to coat.
9. Serve the roasted chicken thighs with the broccoli salad.

NUTRITIONAL INFORMATION:

Calories: 438, Protein: 35g, Fat: 27g, Carbohydrates: 16g, Fiber: 4g, Sugar: 10g, Sodium: 256mg.

PREP TIME: **15 MINUTES**

COOK TIME: **30-35 MINUTES**

RECIPE SIX

ONE POT CREAM MUSHROOM CHICKEN PASTA

A comforting and flavorful pasta dish made with tender chicken, mushrooms, garlic, and cream, all cooked in one pot for easy cleanup. Perfect for a quick and easy weeknight dinner.

INGREDIENTS:

1 pound boneless, skinless chicken breasts, cut into bite-sized pieces

8 ounces sliced mushrooms

1 medium onion, diced

3 cloves garlic, minced

1 tablespoon olive oil

1 teaspoon dried thyme

1 teaspoon dried oregano

1/2 teaspoon salt

1/4 teaspoon black pepper

8 ounces dry pasta (such as penne or fusilli)

2 cups low-sodium chicken broth

1 cup heavy cream

1/2 cup grated Parmesan cheese

Fresh parsley, chopped (optional)

INSTRUCTIONS:

1. Heat olive oil in a large pot or Dutch oven over medium-high heat. Add chicken and cook until browned and no longer pink, about 5 minutes. Remove chicken from the pot and set aside.
2. Add mushrooms, onion, and garlic to the pot and cook until softened, about 5 minutes.
3. Add dried thyme, dried oregano, salt, and black pepper to the pot and stir to combine.
4. Add dry pasta and chicken broth to the pot and stir to combine. Bring the mixture to a boil, then reduce the heat to low and cover the pot. Simmer for 12-15 minutes, stirring occasionally, until the pasta is tender and most of the liquid has been absorbed.
5. Add the cooked chicken back to the pot, along with the heavy cream and grated Parmesan cheese. Stir to combine and cook for 2-3 minutes, until the sauce has thickened.
6. Garnish with chopped fresh parsley, if desired, and serve immediately.

NUTRITIONAL INFORMATION:

4 servings. Per servigng:

Calories: 550, Fat: 29g, Carbohydrates: 39g, Protein: 36g, Fiber: 3g, Sugar: 4g, Sodium: 500mg.

PREP TIME: **10 MINUTES**

COOK TIME: **30 MINUTES**

RECIPE SEVEN

BEEF RAGU

This hearty Italian dish features tender beef braised in a rich tomato-based sauce, served over your favorite pasta. It's a delicious and filling meal that's perfect for a cozy night in.

INGREDIENTS:

2 pounds beef chuck roast, cut into 1-inch pieces

2 tablespoons olive oil

1 large onion, diced

4 garlic cloves, minced

2 tablespoons tomato paste

1 can (28 ounces) crushed tomatoes

1 cup beef broth

1 tablespoon dried basil

1 tablespoon dried oregano

1 teaspoon salt

1/2 teaspoon black pepper

1 pound rigatoni or other pasta

Parmesan cheese, grated, for serving

INSTRUCTIONS:

1. In a large pot or Dutch oven, heat the olive oil over medium heat. Add the beef and cook until browned on all sides, about 5 minutes. Remove the beef from the pot and set aside.
2. Add the onion to the same pot and cook until softened, about 5 minutes. Add the garlic and cook for 1 more minute.
3. Stir in the tomato paste, crushed tomatoes, beef broth, basil, oregano, salt, and black pepper. Return the beef to the pot and bring the mixture to a simmer.
4. Reduce the heat to low and cover the pot with a lid. Let the mixture cook for 2-3 hours, or until the beef is tender and the sauce has thickened.
5. While the beef ragu is cooking, cook the pasta according to the package instructions.
6. Serve the beef ragu over the cooked pasta, topped with grated Parmesan cheese.

NUTRITIONAL INFORMATION:

This recipe makes 8 servings. Each serving contains approximately:

Calories: 446, Total Fat: 17g, , Saturated Fat: 5g, Cholesterol: 89mg, Sodium: 614mg, Total Carbohydrates: 40g, Dietary Fiber: 4g, Sugars: 7g, Protein: 35g.

PREP TIME: **15 MINUTES**

COOK TIME: **2-3 HOURS**

RECIPE EIGHT

BEEF STROGANOFF

A classic Russian dish made with tender strips of beef, mushrooms, onions, and a sour cream-based sauce. Served over egg noodles or mashed potatoes, this dish is comforting and full of flavor.

INGREDIENTS:

1 lb. beef sirloin or tenderloin, thinly sliced

8 oz. sliced mushrooms

1 medium onion, chopped

2 cloves garlic, minced

2 tbsp. olive oil

2 tbsp. all-purpose flour

1 cup beef broth

1/2 cup sour cream

2 tbsp. Dijon mustard

1 tbsp. Worcestershire sauce

1/4 cup chopped fresh parsley

Salt and black pepper, to taste

8 oz. egg noodles, cooked

INSTRUCTIONS:

1. In a large skillet, heat the olive oil over medium-high heat. Add the beef and cook until browned, about 5 minutes. Remove the beef from the skillet and set aside.
2. In the same skillet, add the mushrooms, onion, and garlic. Cook until the vegetables are tender, about 5-7 minutes.
3. Sprinkle the flour over the vegetables and stir until combined.
4. Slowly pour in the beef broth, whisking constantly to prevent lumps. Bring the mixture to a boil and then reduce the heat to low. Simmer for 5-7 minutes or until the sauce thickens.
5. Stir in the sour cream, Dijon mustard, Worcestershire sauce, and parsley. Cook until heated through, about 2-3 minutes.
6. Season with salt and black pepper to taste.
7. Serve the beef stroganoff over cooked egg noodles.

NUTRITIONAL INFORMATION:

This recipe makes four servings. The following nutritional information is per serving:

Calories: 453, Fat: 23g, Carbohydrates: 31g, Protein: 30g, Fiber: 2g, Sugar: 4g, Sodium: 524mg.

PREP TIME: **10 MINUTES**

COOK TIME: **20 MINUTES**

RECIPE NINE

CROCKPOT PORK CHOPS

A classic Russian dish made with tender strips of beef, mushrooms, onions, and a sour cream-based sauce. Served over egg noodles or mashed potatoes, this dish is comforting and full of flavor.

INGREDIENTS:

4-6 bone-in pork chops

1 tablespoon olive oil

1 teaspoon paprika

1 teaspoon garlic powder

1 teaspoon onion powder

1 teaspoon dried thyme

1/2 teaspoon salt

1/4 teaspoon black pepper

1/2 cup chicken broth

1/4 cup balsamic vinegar

2 tablespoons honey

1 tablespoon Dijon mustard

1 tablespoon cornstarch

2 tablespoons water

Chopped fresh parsley, for garnish

INSTRUCTIONS:

1. In a small bowl, mix together the paprika, garlic powder, onion powder, dried thyme, salt, and black pepper.
2. Rub the spice mixture onto both sides of the pork chops.
3. Heat the olive oil in a large skillet over medium-high heat. Once hot, sear the pork chops for 2-3 minutes on each side until browned.
4. Transfer the pork chops to a crockpot.
5. In a small bowl, whisk together the chicken broth, balsamic vinegar, honey, and Dijon mustard. Pour the mixture over the pork chops.
6. Cover the crockpot and cook on low heat for 6-8 hours, or until the pork chops are cooked through and tender.
7. Once the pork chops are cooked, transfer them to a plate and cover with foil to keep warm.
8. In a small bowl, whisk together the cornstarch and water to create a slurry.
9. Pour the juices from the crockpot into a saucepan and bring to a simmer over medium-high heat.
10. Slowly whisk in the cornstarch slurry and continue to simmer until the sauce thickens, about 3-5 minutes.
11. Spoon the sauce over the pork chops and garnish with chopped parsley, if desired.

CROCKPOT PORK CHOPS

NUTRITIONAL INFORMATION:

SERVING SIZE: 1 pork chop with sauce

Calories: 380, Fat: 17g, Saturated Fat: 5g, Cholesterol: 105mg, Sodium: 520mg, Carbohydrates: 15g, Fiber: 0g, Sugar: 13g, Protein: 37g.

PREP TIME: **15 MINUTES**

COOK TIME: **6-8 HOURS IN THE CROCKPOT**

RECIPE TEN

SALMON AND LEEK RISOTTO

A healthy and delicious meal featuring tender salmon fillets served over a creamy risotto made with leeks, Parmesan cheese, and white wine. It's a comforting and satisfying dish that's perfect for a special occasion.

INGREDIENTS:

1 cup Arborio rice

4 cups chicken or vegetable broth

1 tablespoon olive oil

1 tablespoon unsalted butter

1 medium leek, thinly sliced

2 garlic cloves, minced

1/2 cup dry white wine

1/2 cup grated Parmesan cheese

1 tablespoon fresh lemon juice

1/4 cup chopped fresh parsley

Salt and pepper, to taste

4 salmon fillets, skin removed

Lemon wedges, for serving

INSTRUCTIONS:

1. Heat the broth in a small saucepan and keep warm over low heat.
2. In a large saucepan or Dutch oven, heat the olive oil and butter over medium heat.
3. Add the sliced leeks and minced garlic and sauté until tender, about 5 minutes.
4. Add the Arborio rice and stir to coat with the butter and oil.
5. Add the white wine and cook until absorbed, stirring constantly.
6. Add a ladleful of warm broth and cook, stirring occasionally, until the broth is absorbed.
7. Continue adding broth one ladleful at a time, stirring frequently, until the rice is tender and creamy, about 20-25 minutes.
8. Stir in the Parmesan cheese, lemon juice, and chopped parsley.
9. Season with salt and pepper to taste.
10. Preheat the oven to 400°F (200°C).
11. Place the salmon fillets on a baking sheet lined with parchment paper and season with salt and pepper.
12. Bake the salmon for 10-12 minutes, or until cooked through.
13. Serve the salmon over the risotto, garnished with lemon wedges.

SALMON AND LEEK RISOTTO

NUTRITIONAL INFORMATION:

This recipe yields 4 servings. Each serving contains approximately:

Calories: 504, Fat: 18.8g, Saturated Fat: 5.5g, Cholesterol: 100mg, Carbohydrates: 42.3g, Fiber: 1.7g, Sugars: 2.3g, Protein: 38.6g, Sodium: 739mg.

PREP TIME:

The prep time for this recipe is about 5-10 minutes, plus at least 6 hours of chilling time in the refrigerator.

PREP TIME: **10 MINUTES**

PREP TIME: **30 MINUTES**

Note: The nutritional information is an estimate and may vary depending on the specific ingredients used.

RECIPE ELEVEN

HONEY GARLIC CHICKEN

This dish features juicy and tender chicken thighs cooked in a sweet and savory honey garlic sauce. Served with your favorite veggies or rice, this meal is sure to be a hit with the whole family.

INGREDIENTS:

4 boneless, skinless chicken breasts

1/2 cup honey

1/4 cup soy sauce

1/4 cup ketchup

2 cloves garlic, minced

1 tablespoon olive oil

Salt and pepper to taste

Chopped green onions for garnish

INSTRUCTIONS:

1. Preheat the oven to 375°F (190°C).
2. In a small bowl, whisk together the honey, soy sauce, ketchup, minced garlic, olive oil, salt, and pepper until well combined.
3. Place the chicken breasts in a baking dish.
4. Pour the honey garlic sauce over the chicken, making sure each piece is well coated.
5. Bake for 25-30 minutes, or until the chicken is cooked through and the internal temperature reaches 165°F (75°C).
6. Baste the chicken with the sauce every 10 minutes during cooking to keep it moist and flavorful.
7. Once the chicken is cooked, remove it from the oven and let it rest for 5 minutes.
8. Sprinkle chopped green onions on top for garnish.
9. Serve hot with rice, steamed vegetables, or your favorite sides.

NUTRITIONAL INFORMATION:

Calories: 335, Total fat: 6g, Saturated fat: 1g, Cholesterol: 96mg, Sodium: 993mg, Total carbohydrates: 31g, Dietary fiber: 0g, Sugars: 30g, Protein: 37g.

PREP TIME: **10 MINUTES**

COOK TIME: **30 MINUTES**

Note: This recipe can also be prepared on a grill or in a slow cooker for different cooking methods. Adjust cooking times accordingly.

SNACKS
&
DESSERTS

FROZEN HOT COCOA

1⁄2 cup ice cubes

1 packet hot chocolate mix

1⁄2 cup chocolate whole milk, soy milk or chocolate-flavored nutrition drink (such as Boost or Ensure)

Blend ice cubes until the ice looks like the ice in a snow cone. Add hot chocolate mix. Then add milk. Mix well and serve.

Contains about 230 calories and 10 grams protein.

HIGH-PROTEIN GELATIN

3-ounce package of gelatin (any flavor)

1/3 cup dried egg whites (such as Just Whites, found with other baking products in the grocery store)

Note: Don't use liquid egg whites in this recipe.

Follow the directions on the package for making gelatin. Add dried egg whites to the warm gelatin mixture. Whisk gently for 2 minutes until dissolved.

Chill mixture in the refrigerator until it's set.

1⁄2 cup contains about 110 calories and 9 grams of protein.

INSTANT VANILLA PUDDING

1 can (8 ounces) vanilla-flavored Boost Plus or Ensure Plus, chilled

1 packet (4.5 ounces) vanilla instant pudding mix

Mix until smooth.

Chill in refrigerator for about 1 hour.

Contains about 360 calories and 7 grams of protein.

PEANUT BUTTER SPREAD

1 tablespoon non-fat dry milk

1 tablespoon water

1 teaspoon vanilla extract 1 tablespoon honey

5 tablespoons peanut butter (smooth)

Stir together milk, water and vanilla.

When moist, add the honey and peanut butter. Stir slowly until blended. Spread on crackers or form into balls to chill and eat like candy.

Store in the refrigerator.

3 tablespoons contain about 279 calories and 11 grams of protein.

HARD-BOILED EGGS

6g protein

78 calories per medium sized egg

STRING CHEESE WITH WHOLE-WHEAT CRACKERS

1 stick of string cheese

5-6 whole-wheat crackers

Nutritional Values (approximate):

Calories: 150

Protein: 7g

Fat: 8g

Carbohydrates: 12g

VEGGIES & HUMMUS

3⁄4 cup cashews

1 cup walnuts or pecans

1⁄2 cup raisins

1⁄2 cup dried cranberries (or other dried fruit)

3⁄4 cup shredded coconut

3⁄4 cup chocolate chips or M&M's

Mix well. Store in an air-tight container.

Note: Don't give to children under age 3.

1/2 cup contains about 350 calories and 7 grams of protein.

PEANUT BUTTER WITH APPLE SLICES

1 tablespoon non-fat dry milk 1 tablespoon water

1 teaspoon vanilla extract 1 tablespoon honey

5 tablespoons peanut butter (smooth)

Stir together milk, water and vanilla. When moist, add the honey and peanut butter. Stir slowly until blended. Spread on crackers or form into balls to chill and eat like candy. Store in the refrigerator.

3 tablespoons contain about 279 calories and 11 grams of protein.

COTTAGE CHEESE & BERRIES

1 cup cottage cheese (1% M.F.)

1/2 cup mixed berries (fresh or frozen)

Add the cottage cheese to a bowl and top it with the fresh or frozen berries of choice.

This serving size contains about 188 calories, and 28.5g of protein.

WAFFLE WITH TOPPINGS

1 whole wheat waffle

1 tablespoon of maple syrup

1 tablespoon of almond butter

1/4 cup of fresh berries (strawberries, blueberries, raspberries)

Nutritional Values (approximate):

Calories: 300

Protein: 6g

Fat: 12g

Carbohydrates: 40g

TRAIL MIX

3⁄4 cup cashews

1 cup walnuts or pecans

1⁄2 cup raisins

1⁄2 cup dried cranberries (or other dried fruit)

3⁄4 cup shredded coconut

3⁄4 cup chocolate chips or M&M's

Mix well. Store in an air-tight container.

Note: Don't give to children under age 3.

1/2 cup contains about 350 calories and 7 grams of protein.

ROASTED EDAMAME

Toss thawed edamame with a healthy oil (olive or coconut oil) and sea salt and black pepper (optional)

Roast it at about 375 degrees Fahrenheit for thirty (30) minutes.

Stir at intervals

Each cup contains about 18.5g of protein.

SHAKES, SMOOTHIES AND OTHER DRINKS

The procedure for preparing all shakes and smoothies is the same.

» For all shakes and smoothies, simply combine the ingredients, place in a blender and blend them altogether. You can preferably refrigerate them before serving, but this is not compulsory. Keep leftovers in the refrigerator (no more than 2 days) or keep in a freezer for longer.

» You may also put smoothies into a bowl and add toppings to further increase calories and protein. Examples of toppings include: unsweetened fruit, dried coconut, slivered almonds, finely chopped walnuts and pistachios.

VEGGIES

These are a great way to add micro nutrients like vitamins and minerals to your smoothie. Ideas include:

- Avocado (a great way to in crease calories)
- Spinach
- Carrots
- Kale

FRUITS & BERRIES

These give the smoothie a sweet taste and also add nutrients. Ideas include:

- Strawberries
- Bananas
- Pineapple
- Apple
- Orange

SUBSTITUTE NUTRITIOUS LIQUID FOR WATER

Water does not have calories so we want to use liquids like:

- Whole milk
- Half and half
- Soy milk
- Orange juice
- Apple juice
- Cranberry juice
- Pineapple juice

CHOOSE A DAIRY

This is optional but will add extra calories if you choose to do so.

- Yogurt
- Greek Yogurt
- Cottage Cheese
- Ice-cream
- Sherbet

ADD A SEED OR NUT

This is also optional but it a great way to add extra calories. If your blender is not strong enough, make use of nut butter or powdered nuts (like PB2).

- Peanut butter
- Almond butter
- Walnuts
- Almonds
- Flax seed
- Chia seed

ADDITIONAL ADD INS FOR WEIGHT GAIN OR ADDED PROTEIN.

- Protein powder
- Powdered milk
- Honey
- Oats
- Instant breakfast
- Coconut cream

APPLE PIE À LA MODE

1 cup apple pie filling

1/2 cup whole milk, soy milk or rice milk

1 cup vanilla ice cream or non-dairy ice cream

1/2 teaspoon cinnamon

Contains about 550 calories and 10 grams of protein.

BANANA APPLE SHAKE

1 banana

1/2 cup plain yogurt

1/2 cup unsweetened applesauce

1/2 cup whole milk, soy milk, rice milk or vanilla-flavored nutrition drink (such as Boost or Ensure)

1 tablespoon honey

Contains about 400 calories and 9 grams of protein.

BANANA OATIE

1⁄2 cup cooked oatmeal, chilled 1 banana, frozen

1 cup whole milk, soy milk, rice milk or nutrition drink (such as Boost or Ensure, any flavor)

1 tablespoon honey

1 teaspoon vanilla extract

Contains about 330 calories and 8 grams of protein.

CHOCOLATE MILK SHAKE

1⁄4 cup chocolate syrup 1⁄2 cup powdered milk 11⁄2 cups ice cream

1⁄2 cup high-protein milk (see recipe on this page)

Contains about 460 calories and 25 grams of protein.

CHOCOLATE, BANANA AND PEANUT BUTTER SMOOTHIE

1 cup plain yogurt, whole milk, half-and-half, unflavored soy milk or rice milk

1 tablespoon creamy peanut butter 2 tablespoons chocolate syrup

1 frozen banana (or 1 banana at room temperature

+ 3 ice cubes)

Contains about 550 calories and 14 grams of protein.

COCOA ALMOND SHAKE

1 cup chocolate ice cream

2/3 cup whole milk

1 tablespoon almond butter

1⁄4 cup coconut milk

2 teaspoons coconut extract (optional)

Contains about 590 calories and 14 grams of protein.

LEMON SMOOTHIE

6 ounces lemon yogurt (made with whole milk)

1 cup whole milk

1 medium ripe banana

1 teaspoon vanilla extract

Contains about 415 calories and 16 grams of protein.

PEACH FROST

1 envelope vanilla instant breakfast mix

1 cup whole milk

1/2 cup peach yogurt

6 to 10 crushed ice cubes

Contains about 400 calories and 17 grams of protein.

ORANGE SHAKE

3⁄4 cup vanilla yogurt

2 tablespoons powdered milk

1⁄2 cup orange juice

Contains about 300 calories and 12 grams of protein.

PEACH SHAKE

1 can (8 ounces) vanilla-flavored nutrition drink (such as Boost or Ensure)

1⁄4 teaspoon vanilla

1⁄4 teaspoon cinnamon

1⁄2 cup canned peaches, packed in heavy syrup

Contains about 340 calories and 8 grams of protein.

SHERBET SHAKE

1 cup sherbet

1⁄2 cup whole milk, rice milk, vanilla-flavored soy milk or vanilla-flavored nutrition drink (such as Boost or Ensure)

1⁄2 teaspoon vanilla extract

Contains about 300 calories and 4 grams of protein.

VANILLA INSTANT BREAKFAST SHAKE

1 envelope vanilla instant breakfast mix

1 cup whole milk or half-and-half

1 cup vanilla ice cream

Try this recipe with another flavor of ice cream or instant breakfast mix.

Contains about 560 calories and 19 grams of protein.

STRAWBERRY ALMOND SHAKE

1 can (8 ounces) strawberry-flavored nutrition drink (such as Boost or Ensure)

1⁄2 cup tofu

1⁄2 cup frozen strawberries 1⁄2 teaspoon almond extract

Contains about 540 calories and 28 grams of protein.

GREEN SMOOTHIE

- 1 medium avocado
- 1 cup pineapple
- ½ medium apple
- 1 cup spinach
- 1 cup apple Juice

Estimated Calories: 515

PEANUT BUTTER OATMEAL SMOOTHIE

- ¼ cup powdered oats
- 1 medium banana
- 1/2 cup half and half
- ¼ cup peanut butter
- 1 Tbsp honey

Estimated Calories: 730

PINEAPPLE COCONUT SMOOTHIE

- 1 cup pineapple
- 1 medium banana
- ½ cup coconut cream
- 1 cup pineapple juice

Estimated Calories: 525

BLUEBERRY BLAST SMOOTHIE

- 1 cup blueberries
- 1 medium banana
- ½ cup vanilla Greek yogurt
- 1 cup cranberry juice
- 1 Tbsp ground flax seed

Estimated Calories: 465ted Calories: 465

AVOCADO MANGO SMOOTHIE

½ cup avocado

1 cup mango

1 cup milk (1%)

(~320 calories, 12g protein, 44g carbs)

Thank You for Choosing Our High Calorie Recipes Cookbook!

I want to express my deepest gratitude to each and every one of our readers who have decided to embark on their weight gain journey with the help of our cookbook. I understand that gaining weight can be a challenging and personal experience, and I am thrilled to be a part of your transformation.

In these pages, you will find a collection of delicious and nutritious recipes specifically designed to support your weight gain goals. We have carefully crafted each recipe with ingredients that are high in calories, healthy fats, and essential nutrients to ensure you are gaining weight in a healthy and sustainable manner.

I understand that implementing these recipes into your daily routine may require some adjustments to your lifestyle, and we truly appreciate your dedication and commitment to making positive changes. I encourage you to embrace the recipes, experiment with flavors, and make them your own.

As you embark on your weight gain journey, we kindly request that you provide us with feedback on your experience. Your valuable insights, suggestions, and success stories will not only help me improve the cookbook but also inspire others who are on a similar path.

Please be sure to reach out to me and share your feedback, questions, or concerns. I am here to support you throughout your journey and help you achieve your weight gain goals. Your progress, big or small, is a testament to your determination, and we are honored to be a part of it.

I wish you all the best in your weight gain endeavors. May this cookbook serve as a valuable resource and a friendly companion as you nourish your body and reach your desired weight. Remember, good things take time, and we have no doubt that your hard work will pay off.

Warmest regards and happy cooking,

Rachelle K. Sanders

Introducing "From Stick to Thick": Your Guide to Personalized Weight Gain

Dear readers,

I am thrilled to announce the release of our new book, "From Stick to Thick," designed to further support your weight gain journey. This comprehensive guide is your ultimate resource for understanding the principles of weight gain and personalizing your recipes to fit your unique tastes and preferences.

In "From Stick to Thick," we delve deeper into the foundations of healthy weight gain. We provide you with valuable insights into the science behind weight gain and the importance of nourishing your body with the right nutrients. We understand that everyone's body is different, which is why we emphasize the need to personalize your approach to weight gain.

This book is packed with practical tips, useful strategies, and expert advice to help you transform your eating habits and develop a positive relationship with food. Whether you are a picky eater or have dietary restrictions, "From Stick to Thick" will guide you in finding creative ways to incorporate your favorite flavors and ingredients into your weight gain journey.

We will take you on a step-by-step journey to personalize your recipes, showing you how to modify existing meals, choose the right ingredients, and create a balanced meal plan that suits your needs. Our goal is to empower you to enjoy the foods you already love while nourishing your body with the necessary nutrients to gain healthy weight.

As with our previous cookbook, we invite you to share your experiences, feedback, and success stories from implementing the principles and recipes outlined in "From Stick to Thick." Your valuable insights and suggestions will not only help us improve future editions but also inspire others who are seeking to achieve their weight gain goals.

We are excited to be a part of your weight gain journey once again. "From Stick to Thick" is here to provide you with the necessary tools and knowledge to personalize your recipes and make your weight gain journey a truly enjoyable and nourishing experience.

Thank you for trusting us as your guide on this transformative journey. We wish you all the best as you venture onward, and here's to your successful weight gain!

I invite you to share your experience reading this book by scanning the QR code

Warmest regards,

Rachelle K. Sanders

21-DAY HIGH CALORIE MEAL PLAN

WEEK 1				
	BREAKFAST	LUNCH	DINNER	SNACK/DESSERT
DAY 1	Carrot Cake Overnight Oatmeal	Chicken Shawarma Quinoa Bowl	Keto Crockpot Chicken	Yogurt Parfait
DAY 2	Croissant Breakfast Sandwich	Herb Chicken Cous-cous	Vegan Pulled Jack-fruit Sandwich	Apple Pie à la Mode
DAY 3	Chickpea Salad	Mushroom Carnitas Bowl	Chicken Peri Peri	Veggies & Hummus
DAY 4	Vegan Protein Salad	Red Kidney Bean Burger Bowl	Chicken Thighs with Broccoli Salad	High-Protein Gelatin
DAY 5	Keto Pork Pie	Chicken Farro Salad	One Pot Cream Mushroom Chicken Pasta	Hard-Boiled Eggs
DAY 6	Baked Chicken and Rice	Chicken Avocado Salad	Beef Ragu	Instant Vanilla Pud-ding
DAY 7	Vegan Pesto Pasta	Sloppy Joe Casserole	Beef Stroganoff	Peanut Butter with Apple Slices

WEEK 2

	BREAKFAST	LUNCH	DINNER	SNACK/DESSERT
DAY 8	Carrot Cake Overnight Oatmeal	Chicken Shawarma Quinoa Bowl	Crockpot Pork Chops	String Cheese with Whole-Wheat Crackers
DAY 9	Croissant Breakfast Sandwich	Herb Chicken Couscous	Salmon and Leek Risotto	Trail Mix
DAY 10	Chickpea Salad	Mushroom Carnitas Bowl	Honey Garlic Chicken	Lemon Smoothie
DAY 11	Vegan Protein Salad	Red Kidney Bean Burger Bowl	Keto Crockpot Chicken	High-Protein Milk
DAY 12	Keto Pork Pie	Chicken Farro Salad	One Pot Cream Mushroom Chicken Pasta	Hard-Boiled Eggs
	Chicken Farro Salad	Chicken Alfredo Bake	Cocoa Almond Shake	Instant Vanilla Pudding
DAY 13	Baked Chicken and Rice	Chicken Avocado Salad	Salmon with Veggies	Peach Shake
DAY 14	Vegan Pesto Pasta	Sloppy Joe Casserole	Peri Peri Chicken	Frosty Hot Cocoa

WEEK 3				
	BREAKFAST	LUNCH	DINNER	SNACK/DESSERT
DAY 15	Vegan Protein Salad	Sloppy Joe Casserole	Beef Ragu	Yogurt Parfait
DAY 16	Croissant Breakfast Sandwich	Chicken Farro Salad	Peri Peri Chicken	High-Protein Gelatin
DAY 17	Baked Chicken and Rice	Chicken Shawarma Quinoa Bowl	Vegan Pulled Jackfruit Sandwich	Cottage Cheese & Berries
DAY 18	Salmon with Veggies	Cheesy Chicken Noodle Casserole	Chicken Thighs with Broccoli Salad	Instant Vanilla Pudding
DAY 19	Keto Pork Pie	Herb Chicken Couscous	Crockpot Pork Chops	Peanut Butter with Apple Slices
DAY 20	Vegan Pesto Pasta	Mushroom Carnitas Bowl	Salmon and Leek Risotto	String Cheese with Whole-Wheat Crackers
DAY 21	Chickpea Salad	Red Kidney Bean Burger Bowl	Honey Garlic Chicken	Waffle with Toppings

Printed in Great Britain
by Amazon

44144746R00064